LESS KNOWN HEROES OF BIBLE

My Fasting Journal

Alice Jimmy

INDIA • SINGAPORE • MALAYSIA

ISBN 979-8-89277-917-3

CONTENTS

OBED EDOM

Obed Edom was a levites of the family of Merari.He was the son of Jeduthun. Earlier there family was the resident of foreign town Gath. He came with David back to Israel.David decided to bring the Ark of Covenant to Jerusalem from the house of Abinadab. Abinadab son Uzzah died for mishandling the Ark. King David was afraid and did not want to take the ark to Jerusalem but Obed - Edom happily open his house for The Ark.

"The ark of the Lord remained in the house of Obed-Edom the Gittite three months. And the Lord blessed Obed-Edom and all his household." II Samuel 6:11

When David heard that Lord blessed the house of Obed Edom. He regained his strength and took the Ark from Obed House to the city of David and placed it in Tabernacle.

Obed was so in love with God's presence that after King David shifted the Ark from his house to Jerusalem. He decided to move with the ark and Obed-Edom with his sixty-eight brethren, went to the city of David to serve in tabernacle as gatekeeper and worship leader. I Chronicles 16:38

Jeduthun became the chief musician, and Psalms 33, 62, and 77 were sung by his choir. David appointed some of the Levites to minister before the ark of the Lord and to profess [God's name] and to thank and praise the Lord, the God of Israel:"1 Chronicles 16:4. Obed Edom was one of them.

The entire family of Obed Edom served in the house of the Lord. As they continued their service in God's temple, the family of Obed Edom grew in strength and ability for the service of God. (1 Chronicles 26:8.)

Hosting God's presence entirely changed the family of Obed Edom, Earlier they are called Obed- Edom the Gittite, the foreigners to Israel but now they are families of worship leaders in God's Temple

"You will show me the path of life;
In Your presence is fullness of joy;
In Your right hand there are pleasures forevermore.

Psalms 16:11

JAEL – A KENITE

Jael and the Kenites, descendants of Moses' father-in-law, emerge prominently in the biblical account during the time of Deborah and Barak as Israel confronted the Canaanites. In Judges 4:15, Sisera, the Canaanite commander, seeks refuge in Jael's tent after suffering defeat at the hands of Barak. Despite Jael's husband, Heber, having a peace treaty with Jabin, the King of Canaan, Jael discerns the evil in Sisera and, recognizing the opportunity, extends hospitality to him. Yet, in a twist of events, she uses her resourcefulness and skill with tent pegs to execute him, perceiving Israel's enemies as adversaries of God. Judges 5:24 commemorates Jael as "Most blessed among women," acknowledging her unconventional but impactful role in the deliverance of Israel.

Jael's story transcends mere historical narrative; it unveils profound spiritual lessons. Her swift and resolute actions, driven by a deep understanding of the divine purpose, exemplify a responsiveness to the prompting of the Holy Spirit. The urgency of her decision, as situations rapidly unfold, underscores the importance of being prepared to say yes to God when called upon.

It's notable that Jael, lacking conventional weapons, utilized her unique skills and resourcefulness to honor God's will. This aspect emphasizes the idea that God equips individuals with distinct talents, and when prompted by the Spirit, these gifts can be instrumental in fulfilling divine purposes. Jael's story challenges the conventional notion of what constitutes effective tools in God's hands, highlighting the importance of recognizing and utilizing one's God-given abilities.

The lessons drawn from her story resonate with the fundamental Christian principle of following Jesus' example and embodying the commitment to confront oppression and injustice in the world.

"For you were bought at a price;
therefore glorify God in your body and in your spirit,
which are God's."

I Corinthians 6:20

HUR – MOSES COMPANION

In the Book of Exodus, Hur emerges as a pivotal figure, initially noted as a companion of Moses and Aaron during the Battle of Rephidim against the Amalekites. (Exodus 17:12)Hailing from the tribe of Judah, Hur's significance deepens as he is revealed as the husband of Miriam, the sister of Moses and Aaron.

One of the defining moments showcasing Hur's loyalty occurs during the battle, where he assists Aaron in holding up Moses' hands. This gesture symbolizes the interconnectedness of their roles, underscoring the unity required for the Israelites' victory.

Hur's steadfast support for Moses becomes even more evident when he is entrusted, along with Aaron, with leadership responsibilities in Moses' absence on Mount Sinai. Moses reassures the people that "Aaron and Hur are with you," emphasizing their authority during his temporary departure.(Exodus 24:14)

Tragically, Hur meets his demise while courageously attempting to thwart the creation of the Golden Calf. His sacrifice, in resisting the pressure to comply with the popular demand for the idol, ultimately leads to his untimely death. The murder of Hur leaves Aaron susceptible to yielding to the people's wishes.

Despite the tragic end to Hur's life, his faithfulness does not go unnoticed by God. As a divine reward, Hur's grandson Bezalel is chosen to play a pivotal role in crafting the Tabernacle, highlighting the enduring impact of Hur's commitment to the faith and his lineage's connection to the sacred duties entrusted by God. (Exodus 31:1)

"I am a companion of all who fear You,
And of those who keep Your precepts."

Psalms 119:63

BARUCH – THE SCRIBE

Baruch, the faithful scribe of the revered prophet Jeremiah, emerges as a steadfast companion in the tumultuous times depicted in the Book of Jeremiah. In Jeremiah 36:4, we find Baruch shouldering the responsibility of documenting the prophetic teachings, embodying unwavering commitment to the ideals of his master. Amidst moments of despondency, both Jeremiah and Baruch find solace in their shared dedication to the divine message.

As Jeremiah sought refuge from the wrath of King Jehoakim, he entrusted Baruch with the perilous task of delivering his prophecies to the people gathered in the Temple during a day of fasting (Jeremiah 36:6). Undeterred by the difficulty and danger inherent in the mission, Baruch fearlessly fulfilled the command. However, the response was far from repentance; instead, King Jehoakim callously burned the book containing the sacred words. Undeterred, Jeremiah instructed Baruch to rewrite the entire book, a testament to both the resilience of the message and Baruch's unwavering commitment (Jeremiah 36:32).

In Jeremiah 45, a personal message to Baruch reflects the prophet's concern for the well-being of his loyal scribe. The message echoes a profound lesson, urging Baruch not to seek greatness for himself but assuring him that amidst adversity, the Lord will preserve his life as a precious prize wherever he goes.

The narrative further unfolds after the fall of Jerusalem, where Baruch stands by Jeremiah's side as they, along with the remnant of Judah, seek refuge in Egypt (Jeremiah 43:1-7). This demonstration of loyalty amidst hardship underscores the depth of their bond. Remarkably, Baruch holds a unique distinction as the only figure in the Old Testament mentioned to have fingerprints, adding a tangible and distinctive touch to his historical presence.

In conclusion, the story of Baruch intertwines with that of Jeremiah, revealing a narrative of unwavering commitment, resilience in the face of adversity, and a unique historical footnote that sets him apart in the annals of the Old Testament.

"For there are three that bear witness in heaven:
the Father, the Word, and the Holy Spirit;
and these three are one."

I John 5:7

PHINEHAS – SON OF ELEAZAR

Phinehas, the grandson of Aaron and son of Eleazar, emerged as a central figure in a pivotal biblical narrative found in Numbers 25:1-9. Faced with Israelites intermarrying with people from Moab and Midian and worshipping the deity Baal-peor, Phinehas took drastic action to halt the immoral union. Driven by zeal for his God and a desire to quell God's wrath, he entered a man's tent and, wielding a spear, struck down both an Israelite man and a Midianite woman.

This bold act, condemned by some as extreme, proved effective in stopping a devastating plague that had befallen the Israelites as divine punishment. God and King David, in Psalms 106:28-31 and Numbers 25:10-13, commended Phinehas for his passionate defense of the divine honor. He was granted a covenant of an everlasting priesthood, securing a legacy for him and his descendants.

Transitioning from this dramatic event, Phinehas later assumed the role of the third High Priest of Israel after his father's passing, as documented in Judges 20:28. His priestly duties were carried out at Bethel, a sacred location of significance in Israel's religious landscape.

Phinehas' story embodies themes of religious fervor, divine justice, and the preservation of moral integrity. His unwavering commitment to the sanctity of his faith, exemplified by the decisive action he took to confront the threat of idolatry and intermarriage, earned him divine favor. This narrative not only highlights the consequences of straying from God's commandments but also underscores the significance of individuals like Phinehas, who, through their resolute actions, played crucial roles in shaping the spiritual destiny of the Israelites.

Never lagging behind in diligence;
aglow in the Spirit, enthusiastically serving the Lord;"

Romans 12:11

JETHRO – THE PRIEST

Jethro, often referred to as the priest of Midian, played a pivotal role in the life of Moses, exemplifying hospitality, trust, and genuine concern. As a descendant of Abraham through his wife Keturah, Jethro's significance in biblical narratives is underscored by his compassionate actions and wise counsel.

When Moses, perplexed about his calling, fled Egypt, it was Jethro who provided refuge and familial support. Jethro's generosity extended beyond mere shelter, as he entrusted Moses with the responsibility of overseeing his flocks (Exodus 3:1)and gave him his daughter Sipporah. In these moments of vulnerability, Jethro's character emerged as a beacon of compassion, setting the stage for a profound connection between the two.

Upon God's summons to Moses, Jethro selflessly allowed him to pursue his divine path (Exodus 4:18). Subsequently, Jethro's heart was open to embracing the God of Israel when he heard of the miraculous rescue of Israel from Egypt (Exodus 18:10-12). This conversion marked a transformative journey for Jethro, leading him to become not only a father-in-law to Moses but also a trusted adviser.

Jethro's wisdom shone through in his counsel to Moses regarding the overwhelming responsibilities of leadership. Sensing the burden on Moses, he advocated for the establishment of a judicial system to share the workload. Moses heeded Jethro's advice, and with God's approval, a judicial framework was implemented, easing the strain on Moses as he addressed the nation's needs (Exodus 18:17-24).

In this narrative, Jethro emerges as a symbol of compassion, adaptability, and sagacity. His journey from a generous host to a trusted adviser showcases the transformative power of faith and the impact one individual can have on the trajectory of another's life. Jethro's legacy, intricately woven into the fabric of biblical history, stands as a testament to the profound influence of hospitality, trust, and wise counsel.

"Listen to counsel and receive instruction,
That you may be wise in your latter days.
There are many plans in a man's heart,
Nevertheless the Lord's counsel—that will stand."

Proverbs 19:20-21

MIRIAM – THE PROPHET

Miriam, the elder sister of Moses, played a significant role in the early life of the Israelite leader. In the face of adversity, she demonstrated unwavering belief in her brother's destiny. The biblical account in Exodus 2:4 portrays Miriam's commitment as she followed the basket in which Moses was placed, ensuring his safety when abandoned in the Nile River by their parents.

When Pharaoh's daughter discovered Moses and decided to raise him, Miriam quickly facilitated a reunion with their mother, arranging for her to become Moses' nanny (Exodus 2:7). This strategic move showcased Miriam's resourcefulness and her commitment to safeguarding her brother, who would later emerge as the liberator of the Israelites from Egyptian bondage.

Miriam's pivotal role continued during the Exodus, where she led all the women in the escape from Egypt. As depicted in Exodus 15:20, she stood as a prophetess, guiding the women in worship when the miraculous parting of the Red Sea facilitated their escape from Pharaoh's grasp.

However, Miriam faced a challenging moment in Numbers 12:1 when she, along with Aaron, criticised Moses for marrying a Cushite woman. This drew God's displeasure, resulting in Miriam contracting leprosy as a consequence of her words and racist comments. God, in His compassion, acted as a father to Miriam, healing her and demonstrating forgiveness.

Interestingly, in Micah 6:4, God acknowledged Miriam as a saviour akin to Moses, emphasising her role in delivering the Israelites from the bondage of Egypt. This recognition underscores Miriam's significance in the narrative of salvation and liberation.

In summary, Miriam's journey is one of faith, leadership, and redemption. From protecting Moses as a baby to leading the women in worship during the Exodus, Miriam's story reflects resilience, devotion, and the transformative power of divine compassion.

"Let each of you look out not only for his own interests, but also for the interests of others."

Philippians 2:4

BEZALEL & OHOLIAB – THE ARTISAN

Bezalel and Oholiab, chosen by God for the sacred task of constructing the tabernacle, played pivotal roles in creating a dwelling place for the Almighty among His people. Bezalel, whose very name signifies "in the shadow of God," was not just a skilled craftsman but a vessel filled with the Spirit of God. In Exodus 31:3, we learn that God endowed Bezalel with wisdom, understanding, knowledge, and craftsmanship, empowering him for the divine work ahead.

Hailing from the lineage of Uri and the grandson of Hur, Bezalel demonstrated not only exceptional skills but also remarkable humility and submission to his leader, Moses. Despite his expertise, Bezalel recognised the divine authority behind Moses' instructions, showcasing a character marked by humility and devotion. Exodus 39:43 highlights his commitment to faithfully carrying out God's work under Moses' guidance.

Oholiab, a member of the tribe of Dan, shared in the divine favour, being recognised for his wholehearted devotion to God and exceptional abilities. Exodus 31:6 acknowledges the skill and ability bestowed upon Oholiab by God, emphasising his crucial role in the construction of the tabernacle. Both Bezalel and Oholiab stood not only as skilled craftsmen but also as willing teachers, imparting their knowledge to others, as depicted in Exodus 35:34-35.

Their faithfulness extended beyond craftsmanship; Bezalel and Oholiab also demonstrated unwavering dedication in handling the offerings of the people, as revealed in Exodus 36:5. Their commitment to God's work, both in skilful execution and faithful stewardship, played a vital role in the successful completion of the tabernacle.

In essence, Bezalel and Oholiab's narrative serves as a profound example of divine collaboration, where God's chosen individuals, endowed with unique talents, work in harmony to create a sacred space for His presence. Their humility, skill, and devotion stand as enduring lessons for those called to serve in God's grand design, illustrating the beauty that unfolds when human craftsmanship aligns with divine guidance.

"Do you see a man who excels in his work?
He will stand before kings;
No He will not stand before unknown men."

Proverbs 22:29

ELIEZER – OF DAMASCUS

In the biblical narrative, Eliezer of Damascus emerges as a figure of unwavering dedication and loyalty within the household of Abraham. Initially designated as the steward and presumed heir to Abraham, Eliezer's position shifted with the birth of Isaac. Despite relinquishing the assumed role as heir, Eliezer chose a path of respect rather than harbouring bitterness, showcasing a profound commitment to his master and his son (Genesis 15:2).

Abraham, observing that his son Isaac had reached the age of forty without a spouse, took decisive action to secure a suitable bride. Entrusting this crucial mission to his trusted servant Eliezer, Abraham sent him to Haran in Mesopotamia with explicit instructions to find a bride from his own relatives, steering clear of local Canaanite unions (Genesis 24:12). Eliezer, entrusted with the future of Abraham's lineage, became an extension of Abraham's will, demonstrating an unparalleled level of trust bestowed upon him by his master.

Eliezer's journey to find a bride for Isaac is marked by divine guidance and a profound sense of duty. Through prayer and reliance on the God of his master, Eliezer sought a sign. Led by the Holy Spirit, he navigated the intricate task of selecting the perfect bride. In making himself an extension of Abraham, Eliezer drew upon the immense power and merit associated with his master, as referenced in 2 Corinthians 11:2.

The culmination of Eliezer's faithful journey was the encounter with Rebecca, a woman chosen by divine providence to become Isaac's bride. Eliezer, armed with the reputation and trust placed in him by Abraham, approached Rebecca's family with a proposal that transcended mere familial considerations. The family, recognising the association with the esteemed Abraham, willingly entrusted their daughter into Eliezer's care, sealing the union that would play a pivotal role in the unfolding narrative of Abraham's lineage.

In essence, Eliezer's unwavering dedication, reliance on divine guidance, and humble submission as an extension of Abraham exemplify the virtues of loyalty, trust, and selflessness within the context of biblical narratives."

As each one has received a gift,
minister it to one another,
as good stewards of the manifold grace of God."

I Peter 4:10

TAMAR – JUDAH'S DAUGHTER IN LAW

Tamar, a noble lady whose life unfolded in the pages of Genesis 38 and 1 Chronicles 4:1, endured a fate steeped in tragedy and injustice. The demise of both her husbands, attributed to their own wickedness, left her a widow burdened with false accusations. Judah, her father-in-law, wrongly placed blame on Tamar for the deaths of his two sons, Er and Onan. Although initially promised to marry Shelah, Judah's third son, she was left in a state of perpetual waiting as the patriarch failed to fulfill his commitment.

Refusing to resign herself to a life of obscurity and poverty, Tamar displayed a remarkable determination. Rooted in her understanding of the honor tied to the family she had married into, she aspired not only for recognition but also to be considered blessed by bearing godly children. Her steadfastness was evident as she cleverly deceived Judah into impregnating her, a bold move that showcased her assertiveness and willingness to deviate from societal norms.

Tamar's story transcends mere personal ambition; it becomes a narrative of faith and resilience. Despite the judgments of those around her, she remained resolute in her pursuit of acknowledgment, aspiring to be counted among the blessed mothers in the genealogy of David and, ultimately, Jesus Christ. Her unwavering faith caught the attention of God, who blessed her with two sons, Perez and Zerah, ensuring her pivotal role in the continuation of Judah's family line.

In retrospect, Tamar emerges as a figure marked by qualities that echo through generations. Her assertiveness, unconventional approach, and unwavering loyalty to her family set a precedent mirrored in her descendant, King David. Through her actions, Tamar not only secured her place in history but also played a vital role in shaping the lineage that would lead to the illustrious figures of David and Jesus Christ. Her legacy stands as a testament to the transformative power of determination and faith in the face of adversity.

"For He satisfies the longing soul,
And fills the hungry soul with goodness."

Psalms 107:9

HIEL OF BETHEL

HIEL, meaning "life of God" in Hebrew, resided in the sacred dwelling of God known as Bethel. Amidst the rule of the wicked King Ahab, when many deviated from righteous paths, HIEL stood as a beacon of God's character. Bravely defying the curse associated with Jericho, he chose to reconstruct the city, as recounted in Joshua 6:26.

Jericho, situated in the lower Jordan valley, held strategic importance, controlling vital migration routes. Often referred to as the "city of Palms," it boasted fertility and played a key role as a border city. In the time of Jesus, Jericho remained significant, as evidenced in Luke 19:1, being one of the cities near Jerusalem.

Despite Jericho's cursed status, HIEL resolved to rebuild it for the benefit of Israel, dedicating his children to this endeavour. His firstborn, Abiram, with a name meaning "my father is exalted," and his youngest, Segub, whose name signified "fortified," were devoted to this cause.

In a display of profound commitment, HIEL made the ultimate sacrifice. During the foundation laying, he offered his older son, Abiram, and when erecting the gates, his youngest, Segub. This act, detailed in 1 Kings 16:34, not only symbolised HIEL's unwavering faith but also marked the fortification of Jericho, breaking the curse that loomed over the city.

HIEL's courageous decision echoes the resilience and determination to embody divine principles. His actions transcend the boundaries of time, showcasing a commitment to faith and people that defies conventional norms. The narrative of HIEL not only illustrates the historical significance of Jericho but also serves as a testament to the transformative power of unwavering faith and sacrificial devotion.

"And walk in love, as Christ also has loved us
and given Himself for us,
an offering and a sacrifice to God
for a sweet-smelling aroma."

Ephesians 5:2

JEHU – THE KILLER OF JEZEBEL

Jehu, anointed by a son of a prophet sent by Elisha, bore a profound purpose – to obliterate the house of Ahab and avenge the spilled blood of the Lord's servants by the hand of Jezebel. His lineage, as the son of Jehoshaphat, meaning "Jehovah judge," and the grandson of Nimshi, meaning "rescued from danger," carried a generational mantle, signifying a destiny intertwined with divine justice.

Jezebel, infamous for her seduction of God's servants and dissemination of false teachings, possessed a captivating power noted in Revelation 2:20. The biblical narrative underscores that it was solely through the anointing and mantle of Jehu that Jezebel could be vanquished, emphasising the transformative force of divine consecration.

Isaiah 10:27 lends support to the concept that anointing holds the power to break the yoke of oppression. Jehu, ascending as king, executed the entire lineage of Ahab, fulfilling the divine mandate. When confronting Jezebel, she resorted to her old seductive tactics, painting her eyes in an attempt to beguile Jehu. However, fortified by the anointing, Jehu, undeterred, commanded Jezebel's servants to cast her from a window. In alignment with prophecy, Jezebel met her demise, and her blood was ultimately devoured by dogs, as detailed in 2 Kings 9.

Jehu's narrative not only illustrates the potency of divine anointing but also serves as a testament to the necessity of confronting and eradicating spiritual corruption. In this biblical account, the interplay of lineage, anointing, and prophetic fulfillments unveils a narrative rich in spiritual significance and lessons on divine justice.

"For evildoers shall be cut off;
But those who wait on the Lord,
They shall inherit the earth."

Psalms 37:9

JEHOIADA – THE PRIEST

In the tumultuous narrative of the biblical account found in 2 Chronicles, the character of Jehoiada emerges as a pivotal figure in the political and religious restoration of Judah. Jehoiada, a priest hailing from the esteemed lineage of Aaron, played a crucial role in the face of the usurpation of the throne by Athaliah, the daughter of Ahab and Jezebel.

Athaliah's ruthless quest for power led her to commit a heinous act – the massacre of her own sons and grandsons, extinguishing any potential rivals to her rule. Yet, in the shadows of this dark episode, Jehoiada's courage shone brightly. Jehoshabeath, the daughter of the slain king, and the wife of Jehoiada, concealed her brother Joash, the rightful heir to the throne, for six years.(2 Chronicles 23:3)

In the seventh year, Jehoiada, fortified by the support of captains of hundreds and elders of Judah, orchestrated a covenant in the house of God. This covenant symbolized a commitment to overthrow Athaliah's tyrannical reign and proclaim Joash as the legitimate king. Jehoiada's declaration echoed the divine promise concerning the sons of David.(2 Chronicles 23:9-11)

Armed with the weapons of King David, stored in the house of God, Jehoiada strategically stationed the people around the newly crowned king. The solemn coronation of Joash, accompanied by the presentation of the Mosaic Law, marked a pivotal moment in the restoration of rightful governance. The demise of Athaliah and her followers followed, sealing the triumph of righteousness over tyranny.

Jehoiada's influence extended beyond the political realm. He forged a covenant aligning the people with the Lord, fostering a collective commitment to righteousness.(2 Chronicles 23:16)Under Jehoiada's guidance, Joash governed justly, earning the approval of the Lord. Additionally, Jehoiada spearheaded the restoration of the temple and the revered tabernacle of David. (2 Chronicles 24:2,4)

In a poignant conclusion to his impactful life, Jehoiada lived for 130 years and was accorded an honorable burial in the king's tomb. Jehoiada's unwavering faith and decisive actions secured his place as a luminary in the annals of Judah's history.

"and has made us kings and priests to His God and Father, to Him be glory and dominion forever and ever.
Amen"

Revelation 1:6 NKJV

MORDECAI – THE DESTINY MAKER

Mordecai, a prominent figure in the biblical narrative found in the Book of Esther, emerges as a resilient and wise character from the tribe of Benjamin, intricately connected to the lineage of King Saul. When tragedy struck and Esther's parents passed away, Mordecai, recognising familial ties, took her under his wing, assuming the role of a devoted father.

In the face of societal perceptions that deemed Esther a poor orphan, Mordecai discerned her latent potential. He astutely mentored her, perceiving a destiny beyond her humble beginnings. Advising her to conceal her Jewish identity, Mordecai strategically guided Esther into the competitive arena of the King's harem, propelling her toward an unforeseen regal future.

However, Mordecai's commitment to his Jewish heritage became a pivotal point of conflict. When King Xerxes elevated Haman, an Amalekite, Mordecai, anchored in his identity, adamantly refused homage. This act, though an expression of faith, posed a grave threat to the Jewish community. Undeterred, Mordecai turned to prayer and fasting, relying on his unwavering trust in God.

Throughout the unfolding drama, Mordecai's steadfast guidance remained pivotal. He empowered Esther to grasp her authority, revealing a path that would ultimately lead to the salvation of the entire Jewish community. Mordecai's words in Esther 4:14 resonate as a beacon of empowerment, emphasising Esther's divine purpose and the profound impact she could wield.

God honoured Mordecai's determination, positioning him with influence and authority, as seen in Esther 9:4. Mordecai's role extended beyond familial connections; he played a critical part in shaping Esther's destiny as a glorious queen, serving as both mentor and guardian.

In essence, Mordecai's character exemplifies resilience, wisdom, and unwavering faith. His guidance not only shaped Esther's destiny but also became instrumental in the deliverance of the Jewish people, showcasing the profound impact one individual can have on the course of history.

"And let us not grow weary while doing good,
for in due season we shall reap if we do not lose heart."

Galatians 6:9 NKJV

THE QUEEN OF SHEBA

The Queen of Sheba, a powerful ruler of the great kingdom of Ethiopia, embarked on a profound journey to Jerusalem in pursuit of wisdom. Leading a vast caravan, she sought an audience with the renowned King Solomon, desiring to learn the art of governance for her own kingdom. In the historical account found in 1 Kings 10:10, Solomon generously shared his wisdom, patiently addressing her numerous questions.

Recognising the immense value of wisdom, the Queen of Sheba didn't approach Solomon empty-handed. Instead, she brought precious gifts as a token of her deep appreciation for the knowledge she gained during her visit. Her understanding of the blessedness of continuous learning and the significance of wise mentors is echoed in 2 Chronicles 9:7.

Centuries later, Jesus made reference to the Queen of Sheba, acknowledging her journey from the ends of the earth to seek Solomon's wisdom (Matthew 12:42, Luke 11:31). This recognition underscores the enduring impact of her quest for knowledge.

In a spiritual context, the Queen of Sheba's search for wisdom led her to encounter the God of Solomon, who, according to 1 Corinthians 1:30, is personified wisdom in the form of Jesus Christ.

Her journey back to Ethiopia was transformative, as she introduced her kingdom to the worship of the one God she had discovered through Solomon's wisdom.

This profound influence of wisdom is further emphasised in Acts 8:27, where Ethiopian people, inspired by the Queen of Sheba's pursuit of wisdom, find Christ. The wisdom imparted by Solomon becomes a conduit for the Ethiopian people to recognise and embrace the teachings of Jesus Christ.

In essence, the Queen of Sheba's journey becomes a symbol of the transformative power of seeking wisdom. Her encounter with Solomon not only enriched her own kingdom but also played a pivotal role in bringing the wisdom of Christ to the Ethiopian people, creating a lasting legacy that transcends time.

For the Lord gives wisdom;
From His mouth come knowledge and understanding;"

Proverbs 2:6

URIAH – THE HITTITE

Uriah the Hittite, a foreigner in the land of Israel, emerges in the biblical narrative as one of King David's mighty men, renowned not only for his prowess in battle but also for his unwavering loyalty and upstanding character. The name Uriah, meaning "Yahweh is my light," reflects his commitment to the God of Israel, despite his non-Israelite origin.

In 2 Samuel 23:39, Uriah's valour is highlighted, portraying him as a formidable warrior and a man of integrity. His loyalty is poignantly demonstrated when King David, entangled in an adulterous affair with Uriah's wife Bathsheba, attempts to manipulate him into spending time with her. Contrary to David's expectations, Uriah steadfastly refuses the comforts of home, choosing instead to remain devoted to his duty and fellow soldiers.

Despite David's subsequent efforts, including getting Uriah intoxicated, the Hittite soldier resolutely abstains from indulging in personal pleasures. This steadfastness only amplifies the tragedy that unfolds when David, driven by guilt and desperation, orders Uriah's murder to conceal his own transgressions.

The consequences of this fateful decision reverberate through the divine curse pronounced upon David's family in 2 Samuel 12:10.

God, angered by David's actions, declares that the sword will never depart from his house. The blood of Uriah, a man of honour sacrificed for his loyalty, becomes an indelible stain on David's lineage.

The story of Uriah the Hittite serves as a powerful moral tale, illustrating the destructive consequences of betrayal and the profound impact of individual choices on the course of history. Uriah's unwavering commitment to both his principles and duty in the face of deceit stands as a timeless example of integrity. Through the divine retribution that follows, the narrative underscores the inescapable justice that prevails, even when the mighty fall.

"O Lord God, to whom vengeance belongs
— O God, to whom vengeance belongs, shine forth! Rise up, O Judge of the earth;.. "

Psalms 94:1-2

JOHANAN – SON OF KAREAH

Trusting in God amid life's uncertainties is a profound test of faith, a sentiment magnificently captured in the intricate narrative of Johanan, a figure from biblical history. (Jeremiah 40:8, 2 King 25:23) The ease of trusting God during favourable circumstances stands in stark contrast to the formidable challenge presented when faced with an uncertain future, especially when God's path diverges from our perceived optimal solution.

Drawing parallels with Johanan, who warned the appointed governor Gedaliah about the nefarious plans of Ishmael, we find a cautionary tale of prudence unheeded. (Jeremiah 40:13,16). Despite Johanan's foresight and offer to preemptively thwart the threat, Gedaliah, the unsuspecting governor, dismissed the counsel, ultimately leading to his assassination. Johanan, undeterred, pursued the assassin and rescued captives taken by Ishmael, showcasing a commitment to justice and protection of the vulnerable. (Jeremiah 41:8,13,15-16)

Johanan's subsequent turn to the prophet Jeremiah for guidance, in the aftermath of Gedaliah's demise, reveals a genuine desire for divine counsel. (Jeremiah 42:1,8) However, despite receiving clear instructions to remain in the land, Johanan and his associates faltered in their commitment, choosing to relocate to Egypt out of fear of Chaldean retribution. This deviation from the divine directive exemplifies the human inclination to stray from God's path when faced with adversity or perceived threats. (Jeremiah 43:2,4-5)

The enduring lesson from Johanan's narrative underscores the importance of unwavering faith, akin to an anchor steadfast in storm or calm. Regardless of life's uncertainties or the divergence between God's plan and our perceived solutions, maintaining trust becomes a vital anchor for the soul. Like Johanan, we must heed divine counsel, even when it challenges our understanding, and resist the temptation to veer off the path guided by faith.

In essence, the tale of Johanan beckons believers to cultivate a resilient faith, one that withstands the tempests of life and remains unshaken in the face of uncertainty.

"This hope we have as an anchor of the soul,
both sure and steadfast,
and which enters the Presence behind the veil,"

Hebrews 6:19

JABEZ – A BLESSED PERSON

Jabez, hailing from the family of Judah, was given the name "Jabez," which means "he causes pain." It is evident that his birth brought emotional and physical hardships to his mother. In biblical times, a name held great significance, often symbolising one's destiny. However, Jabez chose not to accept this negative prophecy and instead fostered a relationship with God, ultimately becoming more honourable than his brothers.

He became renowned for a heartfelt prayer to God:

"And Jabez called upon the God of Israel, saying,

'Oh, that You would bless me indeed,

and enlarge my territory,

that Your hand would be with me,

and that You would keep me from evil,

that I may not cause pain!'

So God granted him what he requested."

- I Chronicles 4:10

Central to Jabez's narrative is his fervent prayer to the God of Israel, a heartfelt plea for divine intervention and blessing. In his supplication, Jabez implores God to bless him abundantly, enlarge his territory, and keep him from evil, all with the overarching aim of avoiding inflicting pain upon others. This prayer encapsulates Jabez's profound desire to transcend the limitations imposed by his name and heritage, seeking instead a life characterized by honor, integrity, and benevolence.

What sets Jabez apart is not merely the content of his prayer, but the unwavering faith and conviction with which he offers it. Despite the ominous connotations of his name and the adversity he undoubtedly faced, Jabez remained steadfast in his belief in the transformative power of prayer and the inherent goodness of God. His faith was not passive resignation to fate, but an active, dynamic force that propelled him forward on a journey of spiritual growth and empowerment.

Through his unwavering devotion and reliance on God, Jabez emerged as a beacon of hope and inspiration, transcending the limitations of his circumstances to become more honorable than his brothers. His story serves as a timeless reminder of the boundless potential inherent in the human spirit, and the transformative power of faith, prayer, and perseverance in the face of adversity.Like Jabez, we too have the power to defy the odds, rewrite our stories, and forge a path of righteousness and blessing for ourselves and others."

"Ask, and it will be given to you; seek, and you will find; knock, and it will be opened to you."

Matthew 7:7

BARZILLAI AND CHIMHAM

Barzillai the Gileadite stands out in biblical narrative as a figure of remarkable integrity, generosity, and foresight. His story, primarily chronicled in 2 Samuel 17:27,During King David's tumultuous flight from his own son Absalom, Barzillai emerges as a pivotal ally. Despite his advanced age and considerable wealth, Barzillai selflessly provides crucial support to David during his time of need. His decision to assist the king, even at personal risk, underscores his unwavering loyalty and sense of duty.

However, what truly distinguishes Barzillai is his humility and foresight. When David extends an invitation to accompany him back to Jerusalem after Absalom's demise, Barzillai declines, recognising his own limitations due to age. Instead, he selflessly requests that his son Chimham be allowed to accompany the king—a decision motivated by both practicality and a desire to ensure his lineage's prosperity. (2 Samuel 19:31-32, 34-39.)

David, acknowledging Barzillai's wisdom and loyalty, grants Chimham favour and blessing, thereby honouring Barzillai's legacy and ensuring his family's future well-being. At the death bed of David also

King David instructs his son Solomon to show kindness and favour to the descendants of Barzillai the Gileadite, allowing them to dine at the royal table. The significance of Barzillai's legacy extends beyond his lifetime. His descendants, including Chimham, are remembered and revered for generations. References to Barzillai's lineage in subsequent biblical texts attest to the enduring impact of his actions and the favor he earned in the eyes of both God and man. BARZILLAI was so renowned that anyone who married his daughter was honoured to be known by his name.

1 King 2:7. Ezra 2:61, Nehemiah 7:63

The mention of Chimham's habitation near Bethlehem, coupled with historical speculation, further underscores the lasting imprint of Barzillai's influence on the land. The possibility that Chimham received a grant of land from David, which eventually became associated with the site of Jesus' birth, adds a poignant layer to Barzillai's narrative, linking his story to the very foundations of Christianity. (Jeremiah 41:17)

In conclusion, the story of Barzillai the Gileadite serves as a timeless testament to the virtues of loyalty, humility, and foresight.

"... For the children ought not to lay up for the parents, but the parents for the children."

II Corinthians 12:14

RECHABITES – JEHONADAB

The story of Jehonadab, the son of Rechab, and his descendants, the Rechabites were Kenites (descendants of Moses father in law 1 Chronicle 2:55), offers a compelling narrative of obedience and faithfulness. Jehonadab's alliance with King Jehu in the eradication of the worshippers of Baal demonstrates his commitment to righteousness and loyalty to God's commandments. Their joint effort in eliminating the corrupt influence of Ahab's family and the pagan worship practices symbolizes a dedication to upholding divine principles.(2 Kings 10:15,23)

Central to the narrative is the unique commandment given by Jehonadab to his family, instructing them to live as perpetual sojourners, abstaining from building houses, sowing seeds, planting vineyards, and instead dwelling in tents. This directive, though unconventional, underscores a deep-rooted commitment to a nomadic lifestyle and a rejection of the materialism and sedentary comforts of settled life. It reflects a profound trust in God's provision and a desire to maintain purity and separation from the corrupting influences of society. (Jeremiah 35:7)

The Rechabites' unwavering obedience to Jehonadab's commandments, as evidenced by their refusal to drink wine when tested by the prophet Jeremiah, exemplifies their steadfast adherence to their ancestral traditions. Despite living in a society that valued indulgence and pleasure-seeking, they remained resolute in their commitment to abstinence, demonstrating an extraordinary level of discipline and devotion.

God's commendation of the Rechabites and the promise of a perpetual lineage serve as a testament to the value of obedience in God's eyes. Their obedience to their ancestor's commands is not merely a matter of fulfilling familial obligations but is deeply intertwined with their faithfulness to God. By honoring the directives passed down through generations, they uphold the principles of righteousness and remain steadfast in their devotion to God.

The story of the Rechabites offers timeless lessons on the importance of obedience, regardless of whether it pertains to divine commandments or earthly authorities. It emphasizes the rewards of fidelity and the enduring legacy of those who remain obedient to God's will.

"Behold, to obey is better than sacrifice,
And to heed than the fat of rams."

I Samuel 15:22

NICODEMUS

The clandestine meeting between Nicodemus, a Pharisee, and Jesus, the revered teacher from Nazareth, as depicted in the Gospel of John, offers a profound narrative of spiritual seeking and transformation. This nocturnal encounter, shrouded in secrecy due to Nicodemus's fear of his fellow Pharisees, serves as a testament to the depth of human longing for truth and understanding.

Nicodemus, despite his position of prominence among the Jewish leaders, approached Jesus with humility and sincerity, recognising in him a divine teacher with authentic miraculous abilities. In their conversation, Jesus unfolded profound insights about eternal truth, challenging Nicodemus to grasp the concept of being "born again" through water and the Spirit to enter the kingdom of Heaven.

Central to this discourse was Jesus's assertion of his identity as the Son of Man sent from heaven, God's begotten Son, and the promise of eternal life for those who believe in him. The iconic verse, John 3:16, encapsulates the essence of Jesus's message of salvation, underscoring the transformative power of faith in him.

Nicodemus's encounter with Jesus proved to be a catalyst for spiritual awakening and transformation. Despite his age and wealth, Nicodemus was deeply moved by Jesus's teachings, leading him to become a clandestine follower and defender of Jesus throughout his life. His defence of Jesus during the trial in John 7:51-52 and his assistance in Jesus's burial alongside Joseph of Arimathea further attest to the profound impact of this encounter on Nicodemus's life.

In conclusion, Nicodemus's clandestine meeting with Jesus offers a timeless narrative of spiritual seeking and transformation. It serves as a poignant reminder of the transformative power of encountering the divine and the profound impact it can have on one's life journey.

"And those who know Your name will put their trust in You; For You, Lord, have not forsaken those who seek You."

Psalms 9:10

JOSEPH OF ARIMATHEA

Joseph of Arimathea stands as a figure of courage and conviction amidst the tumultuous events surrounding the crucifixion of Jesus Christ. Despite being a wealthy and prominent member of the Sanhedrin, Joseph remained a secret disciple of Jesus, fearing reprisal from his fellow Jews. However, when the pivotal moment arrived, Joseph's faith compelled him to act boldly and compassionately.

In the accounts provided by all four gospels, Joseph emerges as a figure of moral integrity and compassion. He was not swayed by the prevailing sentiment of the Council or the fear of repercussions. Instead, he demonstrated a steadfast commitment to his beliefs and principles. Even though he had not consented to the Council's plan for Jesus' crucifixion, he found the courage to approach Pilate and request permission to give Jesus a dignified burial.

The fact that Joseph of Arimathea, a member of the Sanhedrin, took such a bold step is remarkable. It underscores his willingness to defy societal expectations and align himself with his faith, even in the face of potential backlash. His actions not only ensured Jesus received a respectful burial but also fulfilled the prophecy of Isaiah 53:9, which speaks of the Messiah being buried with the rich.

Joseph's act of compassion did not go unnoticed. Pilate, surprised by Jesus' swift death, granted Joseph's request, allowing him to take Jesus' body and place it in his own new tomb. By providing Jesus with a proper burial, Joseph honoured his memory and demonstrated the depth of his devotion.

Moreover, Joseph's role in securing Jesus' burial highlights the complexity of his character. As a wealthy and influential individual, he possessed the political clout necessary to approach Pilate directly. His ability to navigate the corridors of power speaks to his astuteness and resourcefulness.

In conclusion, Joseph of Arimathea's actions during the crucifixion of Jesus exemplify courage, compassion, and unwavering faith. (Mathew 27:57-60, Mark 15:42-47; Luke 23:50-56, John 19: 39-42)

"That He may seat him with princes—
With the princes of His people."

Psalms 113:8

ANANIAS OF DAMASCUS

Ananias stands out in the biblical narrative as a pivotal figure whose obedience to God's instructions catalysed the transformation of Saul of Tarsus into the renowned apostle Paul. As a devout Jewish man, Ananias lived according to the law of Moses and held significant respect within the Jewish community. (Acts 22:12).His encounter with Saul, later Paul, on the road to Damascus illustrates his unwavering commitment to serving God's will despite initial apprehensions. (Acts 9:9)

Following Saul's dramatic encounter with Jesus, during which he was blinded and abstained from food and drink for three days, Ananias received a vision and a message from the Lord instructing him to visit Saul. Despite knowing Saul's notorious reputation as a persecutor of Christians, Ananias obediently followed God's command. This act of obedience demonstrates Ananias's faith and trust in God's plan, even when faced with uncertainty and potential danger.

Ananias's initial hesitation stemmed from Saul's persecution of Christians, yet God revealed to him Saul's role as a chosen instrument to carry His message to the Gentiles, kings, and the sons of Israel. This divine revelation reassured Ananias of God's sovereign plan and purpose for Saul's life, prompting him to set aside his fears and act in obedience.Acts 9:15

Upon meeting Saul, Ananias prayed for him, and as a result, Saul's sight was restored, he was filled with the Holy Spirit, and he was baptised. Ananias's prayer and spiritual guidance played a crucial role in Saul's transformation into the bold apostle Paul, who fervently preached the message of Jesus and endured numerous trials and tribulations for the sake of Christ's name.

(Acts 9: 12-19)

Ananias's obedience to God's call not only facilitated Saul's conversion but also exemplified the transformative power of faith and the importance of following God's will, even in the face of uncertainty and adversity. Through his actions, Ananias epitomised the role of a faithful servant who played a significant part in advancing God's kingdom on earth.

"Finally, my brethren, be strong in the Lord and in the power of His might."

Ephesians 6:10

DORCAS OR TABITHA

The story of Dorcas, also known as Tabitha, as depicted in Acts 9:36-43, is a testament to the power of faith, compassion, and the transformative nature of good deeds. Dorcas, whose name means "gazelle" or "gracious," exemplified these virtues through her selfless acts of charity and devotion to God.

Living in the port city of Joppa, Dorcas was likely a widow herself, familiar with the struggles and hardships faced by others in similar circumstances. Despite her own challenges, she used her talent in sewing not only to sustain her own business but also to provide clothes and support for many widows in need. Her generosity and kindness earned her a reputation as a devoted disciple of God, admired by many in her community.

Tragically, Dorcas fell ill and passed away, leaving behind a grieving community that had benefitted from her goodwill. As preparations for her burial were underway, word spread that Peter, a prominent disciple of Jesus, was nearby. Recognising Peter's connection to the divine, some of Dorcas's fellow disciples called for him in the hopes of a miracle.

When Peter arrived, he was met with a gathering of mourning widows and saints, all deeply impacted by Dorcas's acts of charity.

They showed him the tangible evidence of her good deeds—the clothes she had made to help others. Peter, moved by the outpouring of love and the tangible impact of Dorcas's actions, recognised her worthiness of resurrection.

In a moment of awe-inspiring faith, Peter prayed for Dorcas and instructed her to rise. Miraculously, she returned to life, a living testament to the power of faith and the transformative nature of good works. Peter's proclamation of Dorcas's resurrection sparked widespread belief in God throughout Joppa, opening the door for further ministry and spreading the message of hope and salvation.

The story of Dorcas serves as a timeless reminder of the profound impact individuals can have through acts of compassion and selflessness. Her legacy continues to inspire countless generations to emulate her example, demonstrating that even in the face of adversity, faith and kindness have the power to bring about miracles and change lives.

**"For we are His workmanship,
created in Christ Jesus for good works,
which God prepared beforehand that we should walk in them."**

Ephesians 2:10

EPAPHRODITUS

Epaphroditus, as depicted in the letters of Paul to the Philippians, emerges as a figure of profound significance, embodying traits of loyalty, sacrifice, and unwavering commitment to the Christian mission. Paul's descriptors of Epaphroditus as a brother, companion in labor, fellow soldier, messenger, and personal caretaker reflect a deep bond and shared purpose between them. Their relationship transcended mere acquaintance, illustrating a profound camaraderie forged through their joint spiritual journey.

Central to Epaphroditus' character is his sacrificial nature, exemplified by his role in bringing supplies from the Philippians. Paul portrays these offerings not just as material gifts but as symbolic acts of worship, pleasing to God. This suggests that Epaphroditus approached his service with a heart fully devoted to God, viewing his efforts as a form of spiritual devotion.

Moreover, Epaphroditus's resilience in the face of severe illness showcases his unwavering dedication to both his mission and the Philippians. Despite his own suffering, he remained steadfast, reflecting the depth of his commitment. The divine intervention that spared him from death not only underscored God's mercy but also prevented Paul from experiencing further sorrow, highlighting the profound impact Epaphroditus had on those around him.

Perhaps most striking is Epaphroditus's willingness to risk his life for the work of Christ. His readiness to put his own well-being on the line for the sake of others speaks volumes about his extraordinary commitment to the Christian cause. In a world often characterised by self-interest, Epaphroditus's selflessness serves as a powerful example of true Christian virtue.

In conclusion, Epaphroditus emerges from Paul's letters as a figure of immense significance, embodying qualities of loyalty, sacrifice, and unwavering commitment to the Christian mission. His deep bond with Paul, sacrificial nature, resilience in adversity, and willingness to risk his life for the sake of Christ's work all serve to underscore his profound impact on the early Christian community. Epaphroditus stands as a timeless example of selfless devotion and steadfast faith, inspiring believers across generations to follow in his footsteps.Phillipians 2:25,26,27,30; 4:18

"And my God shall supply all your need according to His riches in glory by Christ Jesus."

Philippians 4:19

ONESIMUS – THE SLAVE

The story of Onesimus exemplifies the transformative power of Christianity in society, particularly in challenging traditions and unethical practices. Onesimus, a slave longing for freedom and a better life, found himself reluctantly serving Philemon, a wealthy and devout man of God in Colossae. Philemon, known for his hospitality to the Church, was described as being filled with love and faith towards the Lord Jesus and all believers.

Onesimus, seeking escape from his circumstances, fled to Rome where he encountered the Apostle Paul. Through the gospel and the love of Christ, Paul not only converted Onesimus but also became his spiritual father. The once "useless" slave became valuable to both Paul and Philemon, not just as a servant but as a brother in Christ (Philemon 1:10-11, 15-16). Paul urged Philemon to receive Onesimus back, not as a mere slave but as a beloved brother, demonstrating the radical equality and brotherhood found in Christianity.

Paul's plea to Philemon to forgive Onesimus and accept him as an equal reflects the transformative nature of Christian love and forgiveness. Despite Onesimus's past transgressions, Paul offered himself as a guarantee for any debts owed by Onesimus, showcasing the sacrificial love and solidarity within the Christian community.

Through the love of Christ, both Onesimus and Philemon underwent profound personal transformations. Onesimus, once a runaway slave, became a faithful and beloved brother in Christ. Philemon, prompted by Paul's urging and the teachings of Christ, embraced Onesimus not as a slave but as an equal in the eyes of God.

The story of Onesimus challenges societal norms and underscores the radical message of Christian love, forgiveness, and equality. It illustrates how Christianity can bring about profound changes in individuals and society, breaking down barriers and transforming relationships. As Colossians 4:9 suggests, Onesimus's journey from slave to beloved brother serves as a powerful testament to the transformative power of the love of Christ.

"There is neither Jew nor Greek, there is neither slave nor free, there is neither male nor female; for you are all one in Christ Jesus."

Galatians 3:28

THE THIEF ON THE CROSS

The story of the Penitent Thief, as recounted in the Bible, serves as a profound testament to the transformative power of repentance and the boundless mercy of God. In the midst of the harrowing scene of Jesus' crucifixion, two criminals find themselves alongside the Son of God, each responding to their circumstances in starkly different ways.

As described in Matthew 27:38 and 44,. They were rebel as mentioned and may be living for several days in hiding for fear of Romans soldiers but caught and were sentenced for crucification with Jesus. However, a pivotal moment occurs when one of the criminals, moved by Jesus' steadfast demeanour and the knowledge of his innocence, experiences a profound change of heart. In Luke 23:39-43, we witness the remarkable transformation of the Penitent Thief, who, in the face of imminent death, confronts his own mortality and acknowledges his sins before God.

The Penitent Thief's recognition of Jesus as the Messiah and his plea for mercy exemplify a genuine repentance born out of a deep reverence for God. In contrast to his fellow criminal, who remains defiant and skeptical, the Penitent Thief humbly accepts responsibility for his actions and demonstrates a humble faith in Jesus' divine authority. His simple yet profound declaration,

"Jesus, remember me when you come into your kingdom," encapsulates the essence of true contrition and trust in the redemptive power of Christ.

In response to the Penitent Thief's sincere confession and faith, Jesus extends a promise of salvation and eternal life, declaring, "Truly I tell you, today you will be with me in paradise." This assurance of forgiveness and reconciliation offers a glimmer of hope amidst the darkness of Golgotha, affirming the universality of God's grace and the possibility of redemption for all who turn to Him in humility and faith.

The story of the Penitent Thief serves as a timeless reminder of the transformative impact of genuine repentance and the boundless mercy of God. It challenges us to examine our own hearts and attitudes towards sin, inviting us to embrace the gift of salvation offered through Jesus Christ and to trust in His promise of eternal life. Through the Penitent Thief's journey from rebellion to redemption, we are reminded of the profound truth that no one is beyond the reach of God's grace, and that through sincere repentance, forgiveness and new life are freely available to all who seek them.

"But that you may know that the
Son of Man has power on earth to forgive sins"—,"

Mark 2:10

MATTHIAS

Matthias occupies a unique and inspiring position among the disciples of Jesus Christ. Unlike the original twelve who were directly called by Jesus during his earthly ministry, Matthias' journey to discipleship took a different route. However, his story embodies profound themes of faithfulness, perseverance, and divine selection.

Although not initially numbered among the twelve disciples, Matthias faithfully walked alongside Jesus throughout his earthly ministry. He witnessed pivotal moments such as Jesus' baptism, accompanied him during his ministry, and stood by his side at the cross and resurrection. Despite not receiving immediate recognition or being among the inner circle, Matthias remained steadfast in his commitment to following Jesus.

The turning point in Matthias' journey came after Jesus' ascension, during a period of prayer and reflection with the other disciples. It was then that they turned to scripture, recalling Jesus' promise regarding the twelve thrones in the regeneration. (Mathew 19:28) This revelation led them to recognise the need to fill the vacancy left by Judas Iscariot. Matthias, having consistently demonstrated his dedication and faithfulness as a follower of Jesus, emerged as a fitting candidate for this important role.

Matthias' appointment as the twelfth disciple was not based on human ambition or merit but on divine intervention and recognition of his faithful service. Through the casting of lots, God affirmed Matthias' calling and demonstrated his sovereignty in choosing his servants.

Matthias' life as a disciple exemplifies the essence of walking with Jesus. Like Adam walked with God in the garden of Eden, Matthias experienced the privilege of intimate fellowship with the Son of God. His journey underscores the transformative power of faithfulness and obedience in the life of a disciple.

Furthermore, Matthias' legacy extends beyond his appointment as a disciple. He embraced his role with zeal and dedication, actively participating in spreading the Gospel message. Despite facing persecution and ultimately martyrdom, Matthias remained steadfast in his commitment to the cause of Christ.

"just as He chose us in Him
before the foundation of the world,
that we should be holy and without blame before Him in love,"

Ephesians 1:4

BARNABAS

Barnabas, also known as Joseph, hailed from the tribe of Levi and was from Cyprus. He gained the moniker "Son of Encouragement" from the apostles due to his uplifting demeanour. (Acts 4:36-37.) Notably, he sold a field and generously donated the proceeds to support the apostles' ministry. Barnabas played a pivotal role in bridging Saul's (later Paul's) conversion to the apostles, vouching for his sincerity and faith. (Acts 9:27)

For Barnabas was a good man [privately and publicly—his godly character benefited both himself and others] and he was full of the Holy Spirit and full of faith. And a great number of people were brought to the Lord by him. It was Barnabas who called Paul for ministry in Antioch and they together made the church people look like Christ and called Christians"(Acts 11:24-26)

Barnabas remained pivotal in addressing theological controversies, as seen in his involvement in the dispute over circumcision in Antioch and subsequent journey to Jerusalem alongside Paul. Additionally, his role in organising relief efforts for believers in need underscores his commitment to serving others and promoting unity within the Christian community.

(Acts 11:30)

He went to missionary journey with Paul.(Acts 13:2)

However, conflicts arose,in second missionary journey, particularly a sharp disagreement with Paul regarding bringing Mark along on their journey. This dispute led to their separation, with Barnabas opting to sail to Cyprus with Mark.

Despite this disagreement, Barnabas continued his ministry, and in 2 Timothy 4:11, Paul acknowledged Mark's valuable assistance and requested his presence. This gesture signifies a possible reconciliation or at least a recognition of Mark's growth and usefulness in ministry.

In essence, Barnabas emerges as a figure of unwavering support, encouragement, and generosity within the early Christian movement. His actions demonstrate a commitment to fostering unity and advancing the cause of spreading the Gospel, even amidst interpersonal tension.

"Let nothing be done through selfish ambition or conceit, but in lowliness of mind let each esteem others better than himself."

Philippians 2:3

AQUILA AND PRISCILLA

In Acts 18:1-3, the narrative unfolds with the encounter between the apostle Paul and the Jewish couple, Aquila and Priscilla, in the bustling city of Corinth. Displaced from Rome by Emperor Claudius's decree expelling Jews, Aquila and Priscilla embark on a new chapter in a foreign land. Despite the upheaval, they maintain their trade as tentmakers, demonstrating resilience and preserving their identity amid relocation challenges. Paul, sharing their profession, recognises kindred spirits in them, forging a deep bond through their shared occupation.

Their partnership extends beyond commerce into ministry as they join Paul in Syria and later in Ephesus. In Ephesus, they encounter Apollos, a fervent servant of God, who, though knowledgeable, lacks full understanding. Aquila and Priscilla, discerning his potential, mentor him, illuminating the way of God more accurately. This act reflects their commitment to nurturing fellow believers and advancing the Kingdom.

Their journey culminates in Rome, where they establish a home church, embodying the ideal of a couple dedicated to working and ministering together. Their unwavering support for Paul and their commitment to the Lord's work is evident in their risk-taking and sacrificial service. Revered in Paul's letters, Aquila and Priscilla epitomise a power couple advancing God's kingdom through their unity, resilience, and unwavering faith.

Romans 16:3, 1 Corinthian's 16:19, 2 Timothy 4:19

"Two are better than one,
Because they have a good reward for their labor."

Ecclesiastes 4:9

www.ingramcontent.com/pod-product-compliance
Lightning Source LLC
LaVergne TN
LVHW021144160826
845679LV00023B/2047